CSU Poetry Series XLVII

IMPROVISING RIVERS

Poems by David Jauss

Cleveland State University Poetry Center

ACKNOWLEDGMENTS

Some of these poems originally appeared in the following magazines, often in different forms and sometimes under different titles:

Agassiz Review: "Beauty"
Crazyhorse: "Star Ledger"
Denver Quarterly: section iii of "Saint Flaubert"
The Georgia Review: "The Blue Coat"
Indiana Review: "Allegedly" and "Black Orchid"
International Poetry Review: "Hymn of Fire"
Kentucky Poetry Review: "Lazarus"
The Missouri Review: "After the End of the World," "Improvising Rivers," and
    "The Master Musicians of Joujouka"
The Nation: "Elk-Hair Caddis" and "Slow River"
The Nebraska Review: "The Proposition of Any River"
North Atlantic Review: "Diminuendo and Crescendo in Blue" and "Sakhalin"
The Paris Review: "Lemons"
Ploughshares: "Jeanne"
Poetry: "Homage to John Cage," "Never," section ii of "Quotations," and
    "Smile"
Poetry East: "Against Sunsets" and section iv of "Saint Flaubert"
Shenandoah: "The Border," "Cyrano," "The Hatchet," sections i, ii, and v of
    "Saint Flaubert," "Style," and "Vietnam Veterans Memorial"
Southern Poetry Review: section i of "Quotations"

"Last Solo" first appeared in *Mixed Voices: Contemporary Poems about Music,* edited by Emilie Buchwald and Ruth Roston (Milkweed Editions, 1991).

I am grateful to the National Endowment for the Arts, the Arkansas Arts Council, and the University of Arkansas at Little Rock for grants which enabled me to write many of these poems.

I also wish to thank Andrea Hollander Budy, Ralph Burns, Stephen Dunn, Lynda Hull, Bart Sutter, Dennis Vannatta, Dave Wojahn, and Deb and Edith Wylder for their advice and support. And special thanks to Phil Dacey, for help above and beyond the call of friendship.

Published by Cleveland State University Poetry Center
1983 E. 24th St, Cleveland, OH 44115

ISBN 1-880834-15-4 (paper)
    1-880834-16-2 (cloth)

Library of Congress catalog
card number: 95-67573

The Ohio Arts Council helped fund this program with state tax dollars to encourage economic growth, educational excellence and cultural enrichment for all Ohioans.

CONTENTS

I

II

III

IV

For Judy

I

IMPROVISING RIVERS

Nights I cannot sleep
I improvise rivers,
yellow willows

drooping over pools
where trout drowse, their fins
keeping them steady,

and overhead the blue
river of sky, endless,
eddying around islands

of clouds. Lying in bed
I listen to the jazz
of water's passage

over rocks, the rapidfire
arpeggios of riffles,
the walking bass-line

of backwater lapping
fallen oaks, and
threading through it all,

in rhythm as syncopated
as sun and shadow
beneath flickering leaves,

the high horn trills
of cedar waxwings, a bird
I've never seen near

any river. So why
do I drag its sweet song
into this prelude to dream?

Because the last time
I fished the Norfork
two turkey vultures

flapped past, huge wings
slapping the dawn
into submission,

their heads looking scalded
or skinned, red
executioner's hoods,

and because I love
cedar waxwings, the muted beauty
of their gold-gone-gray,

their raccoon-masked eyes
and the quaver in their song,
that courageous admission

of uncertainty. And this river
is not the Norfork or Chippewa
nor any other river I've known

though no doubt these rapids
and that limestone bluff,
the muskrat, hair slicked back

like some fifties rocker,
and the stalking crane,
all rise like photographs

from memory, not will.
The known is their current
but these rivers still flow

beyond the border
of nowhere, that last retreat
for those awake too late,

and just as they carry me
into sleep, I carry them
into each day, so that when I rise

and look in the mirror,
that slowest of rivers,
I can see my face

drifting down the years
like a leaf, and though
I cannot know where

the river is carrying me, or why,
I can hear (soft now,
then softer still)

the music of my passing.

THE BLUE COAT

It's summer in Arkansas, the Cold War is history,
but still I see her, that stranger
thirty years ago in Minnesota, the day after
a Civil Defense filmstrip of Hiroshima,
ground zero: a woman, walking alone,
her overcoat twilight blue,
the landscape around her lunar with snow—
streets, sidewalks, and yards obliterated
by drifts the wind scuffs and swirls, and all
glittering like shattered glass
in the brilliant noon . . . What is a life
but millions of moments like this,
millions of lives entering ours for an instant
then disappearing? So why remember her
when I've forgotten neighbors, teachers, even friends?
Why remember her blue coat, the scarf the wind lifted and waved,
when already, only months later,
I'm losing the little girl who disappeared
so long into the Norfork River
her father's cries were animal. At the sound
my friend and I dropped our rods and ran
around the bend, awkward in our waders
and fear, and found him on his knees
at the river's edge, where his daughter lay,
her lips blue and eyes rolled white.
We didn't know what to say, or do.
We just knelt beside him and watched
as his mouth covered hers, a terrible
kind of kiss, and he began to breathe
for all of us. Slowly the night lowered itself
onto our backs, until the river,
bruised by that black weight,
reflected the first stars, those beautiful
accidents of light. When she woke, I stroked her cheek,
called her *sweetheart*, *baby*, almost
kissed her. Now I've lost everything

but her blue lips, the inhuman
white of her eyes. Yet that overcoat remains,
a blue beyond blue in the detonating light
the day the world began to vanish.
I can close my eyes and see it still,
so beautifully trivial it refuses to mean
less than everything.

THE RIVER

One night I went there late,
my parents long asleep,
and walked along the bank,
the only sounds the slap

of water in clefts of rock
and cicadas, chirring overhead
in trees so thick with leaves
the stars were hid. Each step

might have startled a snake
into quick uncoiling strike
but I was more afraid
of myself. I didn't know why

I'd left my bed to come here
where only a week before
a neighbor boy had drowned,
caught in the current's swirl,

but when I finally found
the beach where whispers said
teenagers swam naked
and even made love, I stripped

and stood there, feeling the breeze
touch me wherever it wished,
then took a breath and dove
into the moon that drifted

on the moving dark. Down I swam
until blood yammered in my ears
its one word *breathe*
and the seconds seemed like years.

But still I stayed, my eyes
strained wide. The only light
was the light I keep, still,
in my head, those nights

I think too much of death.
I tried to put it out
by breathing in the dark
but tasted silt, the rot

of fish and algae, and clawed
my way up. When I broke
the surface, gulping air,
the sudden sky exploded

into stars, and, choking, dizzy,
I swam a moment in the vast
everything that was not me.
If the river was a test,

I didn't know if I'd passed
or failed. I climbed out,
pulling myself up the bank
by a gnarled willow root,

and sat there till my breath
came back and the shaking stopped.
Then I slowly dressed
and started the long dark walk

toward home, where I would steal
into my room, a prodigal son
whose absence no one noticed,
and sleep for years where rivers run.

SLOW RIVER

Every river
is two rivers.
The one curling

like smoke
around islands of birch
and pine, defining

itself in drift
and eddy, the purl of rapids
over rocks. The other

the slow river
beneath the river
from which a turtle rises

like the first thought
of the first man
and takes one human breath

before it returns, the rock
of its back bearing it down,
down where the current

is so slow
time seems a dream
you can wake from.

I confess
I have seen this river
in the dark behind my eyes

and wished I could drift in it
forever, silent, oblivious
to the water above

battering so beautifully
the rocks that live
in both worlds.

ELK-HAIR CADDIS

The line I cast is tied
   not only to the fly
      but to the elk

who heard thunder one sunny day
   and fell, dumb,
      to the hard Montana earth

breathing blood. Such beauty
   on the other end
      of this violence:

the golden fly slowly falls
   through sunshot air
      toward a river

full of reflected trees,
   falls and settles
      softly on the water

with a shiver.

THE BORDER

The morning sun slants
    through the kitchen window
as I drink my coffee and listen

to Miles answer the birdsong
    in the evergreens.
It's easy, sitting in the light

of a day not yet spoiled by failure,
    to forget the country half a world
and half a life away, where night

is just beginning, the sky
    over the Mekong River
bruised black as the border on a map,

dividing the world into darkness
    and light, the two
countries we're all citizens of.

But by the time I come home from work
    the border has crept up the yard
toward the hedge of honeysuckle

and I sit in a lawnchair at the edge
    of the shrunken light,
drink sweating in my hand, and brood

over the lie I told at lunch, the wrong
    I did a friend, the right gesture
that was too late to do anything

but hurt—all the petty failures
    of an average day—
until, for comfort, I call up

the larger shame that soldier felt,
        when I was him,
to see the light leaving

the eyes of the dead. I remind myself
        I have killed no one
today. But still the sky

darkens like a map drawn
        and redrawn on the same
soiled paper, each gradation

of darkness a further border,
        complicating location
and fear. To play music now

would be one more betrayal
        so I sit in a silence made larger
by the cry of crickets. Then

the light is gone
        and I'm in that other country
where nothing is clear, where the border

is everywhere.

STYLE

*James P. Johnson, The Jungles Casino, New York,
    February, 1909*

For years he's turned out the lights
and played in the dark, all the keys
black now, so black he knows them in a way
his mother, practicing her Methodist hymns
and cotillion songs on Sunday afternoons,
cannot imagine. And he's covered the keys
with a white sheet and played scales through it
until he could forget it was there, his hands lost
in the long drift of snow. And now, just fifteen,
he's playing a cellar "dancing school," furnace blazing
at his back, the smell of the coal bin and ash heap
thick as the smoke cleaving to the bare rafters.
Under its blue spotlight, the dance floor
moons empty: the "pupils," mostly Gullah longshoremen,
drink in corners with sleepy-eyed whores
or play cards at scarred tables, their talk African
when someone cheats. Outside, Hell's Kitchen
is freezing, snow swirling, wind rattling the windows
between waltzes and two-steps. He tries
one of the schottishes his mother taught him
and a couple begins to dance, but before the song ends
they stop and kiss. The man runs his broad hand
down the curve of her buttocks, and the crowd hoots.
Jimmy blushes. This isn't the way it is
for real ticklers, real ticklers *own* the room:
he thinks of Abba Labba strolling to the piano,
his trademark Homburg tilted to one side, three gold buttons
on the band. The way he'd lay his silver-headed cane
on the music rack, then dust the stool
with his silk handkerchief! And Fred Tunstall
whose Norfolk coat had eighty-two pleats in the back
so that when he bent over the keys
the pleats fanned out like a peacock's tail.
That was style. But he's just a kid

wearing his father's shiny blue serge suit,
he'll never be anybody. So what if he can rag
the *William Tell Overture* or Rachmaninoff's
Prelude in C Sharp Minor? . . . "Take us back home!"
one of the Gullahs calls out. They miss the Carolinas,
the old-fashioned ring shouts, so Jimmy starts to play
"The Spider and the Bed-Bug Had a Good Time."
The Gullahs form a circle around a young woman
and shuffle and clap, laughing and talking until Jimmy
hunches over the piano and, shutting his eyes,
turns out the lights, strikes a black chord
and holds it with his pedal until it rings,
then runs arpeggios up and down the drifting keys,
shifts into a set of modulations as casually
as asking what's for dinner, and strides
into a bluesy stomp, his hands striking
like rattlesnakes. He's not there anymore,
no one's there, not even the dancers standing now,
suddenly silent, staring at him and listening
to the notes fanning out into the room like pleats.

DIMINUENDO AND CRESCENDO IN BLUE

i.

BILLIE'S BLUES

Billie Holiday, Fox Theater, Detroit, 1937

There was nothing the Count could say:
he'd signed a contract. Somebody might think
I was white if the spotlight hit me
just right. Or, rather, wrong. "Or a chink,"

the theater manager said. "She looks yellow
beside you coloreds." There's no damn business
like show business. Fine and mellow,
shit. I was mad. They painted my face

black as my mood. The white girls pranced
around the stage in masks and mammy dresses,
the cats in the band stared straight ahead.
Nobody said nothing, not even Prez,

but when we finished, Basie hugged me, tight.
"It's okay," I said. My voice sounded white.

ii.

ALBINO RED

Red Rodney, Spiro's Beach, Maryland, 1950

Bird's agent threw down his hat. "A Yid
in a black band down south? Are you on dope?"
But Bird only grinned. The sign outside
the tour's first gig: THE KING OF BEBOP

CHARLIE PARKER AND HIS ORCHESTRA, FEATURING
ALBINO RED, BLUES SINGER. Robert Chudnick,
a.k.a. Red Rodney, flips. He can't sing
and who's going to believe he's black?

Everybody, that's who. Drunk, bourgeois,
the crowd cheers each song, not one a blues.
Then Red does that delta classic, "Hava Nagilah."
Woozy, a woman says, "Don't Jews

sing this too?" Her boyfriend nods. "That figures.
Who else would steal a song from niggers?"

iii.

ENTR'ACTE

Miles Davis, Ronnie Scott's Jazz Club, London, 1969

So in comes Miles with his entourage—
you know, girlfriends, bodyguards,
barber, shoeshine boy—and sits right down front.
He's so cool he's wearing sunglasses
though the joint's as dark as his ass.
Professor Irwin Corey—"The World's
Foremost Authority"—stammers, upstaged.
Every joke he cracks earns a rimshot grin

and muttered *shit*. Until, in a blink,
he bends down and whips the shades
off Miles and puts them on his own white face.
For a second, no one even sips a drink.
"No wonder you're smiling," he ends his act.
"With these on, everyone looks black."

iv.

THE WORLD COMES TO THE RESORT HOTEL POOL
IN FRENCH LICK, INDIANA

Dizzy Gillespie, 1958

Surrounded by whites, he struts in, sporting elfin
slippers, green and gold, embroidered by Turks,
his loins girded with crimson bathing trunks
from the Côte d'Azur, towel emblazoned SHERATON

draping, like a sultan's cape, his shoulders
and fastened over his chest with a jade
Egyptian scarab pin. Chinese cigarette holder,
etched with dragons, in one hand, German radio

dangling from the other. Skullcap courtesy
of Greece, sunglasses wraparound, Italian.
Behind the dark lenses, his eyes (South Carolinian)
survey, with plenipotentiary cool,
swimmers treading water like history:
"I've come to integrate the pool!"

BLACK ORCHID

Miles Davis, New York, August, 1950

for Lynda Hull

Tonight he's playing the Black Orchid,
the old Onyx where before his habit
he played with Bird, looking cleaner
than a motherfucker, Brooks Brothers suit,
marcelled hair, trumpet floating over
that hurricane of sixteenth notes no one
could have played sober—19, a dentist's son,
on stage with *Bird* and laying down shit
nobody ever heard before or since!—but now
his fourth cap of heroin's wearing off,
its petals closing up inside his chest so tight
he can barely breathe. Drunk again,
Bud hangs heavy over the keys, left hand
jabbing chords that break his right hand's
waterfall arpeggios: "April in Paris,"
and that strangely tropical odor of coconut
and lime in rum comes back to Miles,
the smell of Paris, Juliette Greco's sweet lips
as she sang, each syllable a kiss
for him alone. *Juliette,*
his trumpet moans, *her small hands*
on the small of my back, long hair black
on the white pillow . . . Even Sartre
tried to talk him into marrying her
but he'd gone back to America, to Irene,
and a habit. And though numerology proved
he was a perfect six, the Devil's number,
he drove the Blue Demon, top down, to East St. Louis,
Irene silent beside him, the kids crying
in the back seat, one thousand miles
to escape heroin and the memory
of Juliette's white shoulder. But now
he's back, alone, long sleeves

hiding fresh tracks on his forearms,
and it's not Bird but Sonny who's unraveling
the melody, looking in it for a way
to put it all back together again.
Then Wardell leaps in, *This is it, man,
can't you* hear *it?* They're dueling
like Ground Hog and Baby, the junky tapdancers
who buck-and-winged for dope on the sidewalk
outside Minton's, feet turning desperation
into music, and Miles joins them, his mute
disguising the notes he fluffs. He sounds
as bad as Fats, last May when they recorded
Birdland All-Stars. Glassy-eyed, nose running,
Fat Girl had to strain to hit notes
he used to own. 26 and just two
months to live. *I'm going to kick this shit,*
Miles vowed the night Fats died,
but here he is, blowing a borrowed horn
because he pawned his own to play
a syringe's one-valve song. If only
he'd stayed, if only he'd never come back . . .
Behind him, Art plays Paris dark
as a jungle, and Miles falls into her pale arms,
the dark hotel room, and he's lost, lost
and free, released from some burden he's borne
across the ocean, to this bed, this woman,
a burden that, lifting, lifts him
like music, one clear unwavering note piercing
the silence that defines it . . .
When he tries to explain, she tells him
that's *existentialisme.* "Existential,
shit," he says, "Let's fuck."
And she laughs, her mouth a red flower
opening under his. Then he kisses
two whole notes out of his horn, their beauty
painful as they vanish into the swirling
smoke of the Orchid, each note
unfurling, an orchid itself, its petals

falling and settling on the nodding heads
of grinning white Americans
who will never understand jazz, or Paris,
or him. He closes his eyes,
and for as long as his solo lasts,
it's not August, it's not New York,
and he is not dying.

LAST SOLO

Charlie Parker, Hotel Stanhope, New York,
March 12, 1955

for David Wojahn

He lies on the sofa, listening to Nica talk
to her daughter in the next room,
his shirt sweat-soaked despite the glass
after glass of ice water he's drunk
to cool the flames in his gut, the ulcers
that will help his heart kill him tonight
as he laughs at a juggler's antics
on *The Tommy Dorsey Show,*
and wishes not for whiskey or the chill
of heroin in his veins, nor for the buzzing jazz
of phenobarbital, but for his saxophone
which Dr. Freymann said could kill him
as surely as any drug. He closes his eyes
and the exhilaration of the illicit
drives the notes down their dark syllogism
of sabotage: he knows he is about to die
a scandalous death, a black man in the suite
of a white baroness, and he knows Chan,
his wife, will never forgive him
but he can't help it, he won't die
like just anyone, he wants to shove his death
into everybody's face. He closes his eyes tighter
and plays on, dismantling melody
and breaking music down to its essential wail;
beyond bop, he blows down the walls
of Bellevue, Camarillo, even the Village clubs
where he imagines Chan, her black pageboy uncombed,
beaver coat unbuttoned, searching for him. *Pree,*
he thinks then, *her tiny face,* and freefalls
as far as his breath will take him, fast
as gravity, the riffs sadistic in their skid
through discordant keys, the notes

shards of glass in his throat; he plays
the telegrams he sent Chan from Los Angeles,
plays MY DAUGHTER IS DEAD STOP
I KNOW IT STOP MY NAME IS BIRD STOP
I AM YOUR HUSBAND STOP HELP STOP . . .
He wants to obliterate all feeling, all self,
all music—to play until there is nothing
left to play, until the silence
is finally empty. Lying there, refusing
to open his eyes to the luxurious furniture
and Oriental rugs, he wishes he could play
the end of the world, and play it so well
that when Nica finds him sprawled on the floor,
his hands choking the neck of his sax,
she will know *this is it, baby,*
this is what music is all about,
and you will never hear its like again.

THE HATCHET

Thelonious Monk, "Round Midnight," New York,
April 5, 1957

Years later, at Bellevue, he'll paint
    the still life Mingus mentions
in *Beneath the Underdog*, an apple

and a hatchet on a background black
    as the night Nellie committed him,
the blade in angular love

with the round apple, its silver edge
    ever so barely touching
the blood-red skin. But now

he sits at the piano, sweating,
    cigarette smoke a noose
unraveling around his neck, and plays

the chart he's played a thousand times
    but never twice. Once he said
there were two kinds of notes, the wrong ones

and those that don't sound as good.
    These are the wrong
wrong notes. He stops, wipes his brow. "Selection

Three, Take Seven," the intercom crackles:
    Orrin Keepnews, producing
Thelonious Himself, the master accompanied

by silence. But Monk's not listening,
    he hears only a ruin
so blue and vast he could call it,

if there were words where he is,
    sky. There are two kinds
of silence, too. He cocks his head to hear

which one he's playing . . .
How the hatchet
envies the sunlight, the way

it splits the apple in half
without violence. If only
it could sleep inside the white

heart of the apple
without destroying it,
if only midnight could be painted

without obliterating the white canvas . . .
His fingers hover,
trembling, over the keys

and the cracks between them
where the notes he's looking for
reside, the right notes

that can only be played
by refusing all others.
He's playing them now, head nodding,

foot tapping, the strain of listening
making him grimace
like a man crazy, or in love.

HYMN OF FIRE

John Coltrane, Huntington Hospital, Huntington,
New York, July 17, 1967

Once he told Elvin, *If we only knew*
the right notes, we could eliminate all friction
in the universe, and all matter would fall
away from itself, nothing would hold anything
together. Later he chanted the seven breaths

of man—*A um ma ni pad me hum*—as if breath
were spirit and body the mere instrument
it played. Meanwhile, each night the news
got worse: riots at Fisk, Jackson State, Texas Southern,
and now twenty-five brothers in Newark have fallen

and the ghetto's ablaze. Everything's falling
apart, the country, himself, and music is a fire
that can neither purify nor destroy . . . He breathes
slowly, carefully, open-mouthed, the cancer
in his liver making each breath a new

reminder of what his music foreknew:
the desire to live forever is the darkest fire,
a fire that cannot cancel the Fall
or its aftermath, though it consumes
everything but the spirit, the breath

he releases now, the seven breaths
become one at last in the final
blissful, burning rise and fall
of his chest, a last hymn
so ancient and eternal it's new,

as he falls, like Newark, in flames, breathless.

THE MASTER MUSICIANS OF JOUJOUKA

Ornette Coleman, Joujouka, Morocco, January 17, 1973

The former Jam Jiver from Fort Worth
who played "Stardust" at the white school's prom
and, later, Uncle Tommed the blues for shake dancers

in Silas Green's New Orleans minstrel show;
and later still, a young Methodist Jesus,
bearded, hair curled in a croquignolle,

thrown off bandstand after bandstand
and beaten, once, in Baton Rouge
for playing *strange*; mocked, too, in L.A.

for his white plastic alto, the instrument
Parker played at Massey Hall, the Greatest
Concert Ever, a toy to those who refused

his request to sit in, just one song, please;
and the elevator "boy" at Bullock's,
pressing the emergency stop button

to study Slonimsky; the divorced husband
who wanted to be a man, not a male,
and begged his doctor to castrate him; even the composer

of freedom—he—no, *they*—have disappeared:
someone else is here, recording
at the festival of Bou Jeloud,

the Muslim Lupercalia. Villagers
dressed in white caftans coil and whirl,
frenetic as the bonfire's light, to the raitas

and drums, the wooden flutes and gimbris,
of the family that since the thirteenth century
served as court musicians to the sultans,

while Bou Jeloud, the wildman in black goatskins,
sows panic, lashing out, baring red teeth.
Every woman he whips with his switch will bear

a child this year . . . Ornette's so far
inside this music, this past that's
more present than the present, he's lost

his own past and the future it dreamed. So when
a tribesman, frothing at the mouth,
dashes howling past the horn mikes,

the Doppler effect's a concise history
of his or any life, its moral
long arrival followed by longer loss,

and he echoes it, his face now dark, now firelit,
with his sax's harmolodic moan. He knows
tomorrow he will have to return

to New York, so he holds the howl
as if it can never fade, as if he's free
of time's gravity, free finally, and home.

AFTER THE END OF THE WORLD

Sun Ra and His Intergalactic Research Arkestra, Berlin, 1976

The Arkestra glitters in their Saturn gowns
and galaxy caps, cosmic rosaries round their necks.
Dancers, acrobats, a fire-eater.
Beside Sun Ra's organ, a telescope on its tripod,
aimed toward the stars beyond the ceiling
he wills to lift off, like a spaceship. Squinting
one eye, opening wide the other. *Welcome*
to the eighth ring of Saturn,

home sweet home. Snickers. If only
they could hear his *Music from the Private Library*
of the Creator of the Universe, they'd know
how homesick he was. He'd recorded it twice
but the tape stayed blank. It was His property,
he could dig that. Forbidden fruit.
Solaristic Precept Number Two: The sequence of life
is sound diminished to its smallest point:

silence.
The smell of butter rum Lifesavers: Coltrane
here again. 1959, the Sutherland Lounge in Chicago,
reading his precepts, laughing but not laughing too
and later playing, now and then,
scattered phrases from the *Private Library*. A citizen
of the universe. *Welcome, John.*
Take a seat in the Eternal Thought

and listen to the Future with us.
Solaristic Precept Number One: Thorough consideration
of the patterns of the past because coming events
cast their shadows before. That's why
you have to give up your life
before you die. Anybody can give it up and die
but to keep on living after, that's the test,
ain't it, John? Pythagoras,

Tycho Brahe, Galileo,
all of them medicine men from outer space
who died into new lives. Behind him the Arkestra finishes
"It's After the End of the World," and he rises,
a black sun, to bow and bless the Berliners who do not know
the impossible is possible because the impossible
is a thought and every thought
is real. *I've come from Saturn*

to make you citizens of Infinity.
How else could he, a boy of seven in Birmingham,
the first time he saw music, play it?
John, you could tell them, if only you could speak
once more on your saxophone, if only
the future weren't so loud
it deafens everyone
doomed to life on this planet.

ALLEGEDLY

darkness was on the face of the deep,
and the firing pin on the boy's .38
was broken, and God divided

light from darkness, and the owner
of Downtown Liquor emptied
his revolver into the boy's face and chest,

then pulled out the shotgun
from under the counter, and the light
He called Day and the darkness Night,

and since the boy died before sunset
it was day, technically,
when his mother left work and drove

not to the hospital to join her husband
but home, where she removed, one by one,
the blankets from their bed, the sheets

and mattress cover, then dragged
the mattress onto the floor and crawled
under its dark weight, and stars

appeared in the firmament, the sun
and moon also, and great whales
surfaced in the sea, birds wheeled

in air glittering with insects,
and cattle lowed in billowing fields,
and when the boy's throat gurgled—

not a word or breath but gas rising
from his blasted guts—the med student
jumped and put her pale hand

to her own throat, and God said
Let us make man in our image,
and the boy stiffened on the bloodstained gurney

while his father knelt, weeping, in the hallway
and his mother moaned beneath the mattress
she wished would crush her, and across town,

the night lit now with neon,
the local hero reloaded, his fingers trembling,
and God saw everything that He had made.

SMILE

The posthumous shock when the bulb flashes,
a kind of time travel—you see
your face displayed, decades from now,
on a flea market table, a stranger's eyes

drifting over it as he passes by.
Your absence, you realize, will be as puny
as your thumb-sized image on the sepia paper,
there will be no one who remembers you

as anything but a name in the family Bible,
and suddenly you envy, with something like thirst,
the photographer, whose absence is as vast
and pure as God's, who created the world,

the story goes, with the same trick of light
and stands now, and forever,
behind the camera, outside
the framed world, squinting at the evidence

that you, for one flash of time, existed.
And you feel rise swirling in you like dust in sunlight
the desire to be so perfectly absent
you could never die.

THURSDAY AFTERNOON AT THE OFFICE

To be that lost. Pines, birches. A deer's white scut
disappearing. Rocks scattered like knuckles,
kneecaps. The river bearing time away, its will
obliteration. If he could follow, what

(not who) would he be? A nun once told him
after Peter denied Christ his tears wore grooves
in his cheeks. He wants to believe
she believed. He wants to affirm

the miracle of denial, each tick of the clock a no
to who he was. But outside his thermopane window
traffic stalls. The phone rings. Who shall he say he is
today? His work? The quintessence of dust?
The phone rings and rings. The forecast is for snow,
enough to make the drive home dangerous.

JEANNE

The insistent logic of rain makes you turn
from the window and try once again to read
the book that made you cry when you were thirteen,
the age the Maid of Orléans saw St. Michael
ride down from the flaming sky and tell her
to mind her mother and always be a good girl.
You read how Jeanne traded her peasant dresses
for boy's clothes and the Dauphin's armor
and, eventually, flames, but the words are cold now—
or is it you?—and you think more about the author
than the girl whose visions sent you into the woods
behind the farmhouse in search of angels
who knew your name. You see her sitting
at her desk, bespectacled, hair in a bun, a finger
lazily twisting one loose strand—as you are twisting
your own—and yawning over some tortured
medieval prose. Was she in love then
or ever? Did her heart burn when Jeanne
gazed heavenward and smiled despite the flames
blistering her charred legs? You doubt it.
Whoever the author was, or is, she did not imagine you,
at thirteen, sobbing into your hot pillow because
St. Michael would not appear. Nor you now, at forty-two,
reading a saint's life in search of the girl
you once were, or hoped to be.

You let the book fall onto your lap and turn back
to the rain-streaked window. The rain
is coming down harder now, and as far as you can see
nothing, anywhere, is burning.

WINGS OF DESIRE

Because this is a movie, the angels have bodies
　　but we know they are only metaphors
　　　　for the soul's longing to be physical:

Bruno Ganz, looking in Wender's black and white
　　like a dissipated preacher,
　　　　gazes at the trapeze artist, alone

in her squalid trailer only moments
　　after the circus has gone bankrupt,
　　　　brushing her long blonde hair

and he wants, not her
　　but the feel of her hair, the heft
　　　　of the brush in his hand, even

her sadness, the wash of it
　　through muscles exhausted
　　　　by her defiance of the ground

beckoning beyond the net. She sighs
　　and he wonders if the soul grows
　　　　when an angel takes on a body

or shrinks, imploding like a star
　　whose gravity is too great
　　　　for light to escape. It is a question

no one can answer for him, not the suicide
　　on the hotel roof, not the lovers
　　　　in their brilliant private dark,

not Nick Cave and the Bad Seeds,
　　spectral, strutting their 4/4 angst,
　　　　not even God, who exists

only in questions about His absence,
or Peter Falk, who plays an angel
pretending to be an actor

named Peter Falk. He cannot know
until he falls into time, the technicolor
misery of Berlin and its New Wave slums,

and sees, high above him,
his beautiful trapeze artist, her back arched
and arms spread wide, flying.

CYRANO

How we admire Cyrano's suffering,
    his noble silence, the purity
of a love kept secret, as he whispers

into the ear of his dying rival
    It's you she loves. Unwitnessed,
his lie wins him neither praise

nor Roxanne, for goodness is nothing
    if not a form
of privacy. But what if he believed

God was watching, as all-knowing and voyeuristic
    as a moviegoer?
An audience taints every good act, a judge

corrupts it utterly. So faith is the greatest obstacle
    to virtue? I'm falling
through this thought when I hear her,

a woman two rows down,
    weeping so loudly I suspect
a grief too personal to be expressed

except in public. Hands over her face,
    she whips her head back
and forth, as if saying *no* over and over

to someone not there. Or is she
    talking to her life? Sympathy
is one disguise curiosity wears:

if I comfort her, I wonder, would she tell me
    the sorrow that sits down with her
each day for dinner, the pain

that makes her bed each morning?
    I believe she would, and I'm tempted
to be the audience that would give her grief

its twist of pleasure. But I turn back
    to the movie and try not to listen
as her sobs gradually subside. In an hour

we sit through twenty-seven minutes of darkness—
    the black spaces between frames—
and though we can't see it, we feel it

behind the images light casts
    on the blank screen: the blue sky,
the green lawn, and Roxanne's face,

beautifully ignorant, as Cyrano, old now
    and dying, visits one last time,
his secret the only thing

holding him, and us, up.

IV

SAKHALIN

Chekhov, August 13, 1890

"We should make pilgrimages to Sakhalin
the way Turks go to Mecca,"
he wrote Suvorin in the first throes

of *mania Sachalinosa.* Ten thousand versts
across Siberia, four thousand by carriage
and "the wicker basket," a drafty, springless tarantass

pulled by two horses whose harness bells
became the theme of his migraines.
Two pairs of trousers and a leather greatcoat

and still he shivered so much he strained
muscles in his back and neck. Coughing blood
from consumptive lungs. Each rut the carriage hit

torturing his hemorrhoids. And day after day, rain
until the Irtysh flooded, its current so swift
the ferry's huge oars could barely claw

their way across, bitterns calling all the while
and icefloes drifting past. And when, back on land,
the wheels sank shaft-deep in the mire

he walked to lighten the horses' load.
Trudging through the mud, the Siberian plain vast
as the sky around him, lost in pain and fatigue,

he forgot, happily, Moscow and its parlors,
steam baths, and literary talk, his summer dacha
and apple orchard, and dreamed of Sakhalin,

the island where Mother Russia's criminal sons
paced in dark cells or slaved in mines, chained
to wheelbarrows. He'd had enough

of comfort, its deathly pallor. He wanted
to tour hell, smell the sulphur
in human nature. And now, after three months

of traveling by train, boat, carriage, and foot,
he's here, in Dué prison, witnessing
the flogging of a man who killed a Cossack

and his grandchildren. Outside,
convicts trek through the courtyard
to their dark day's work, the clank of their chains

like the wicker basket's bells. Yawning,
the German doctor examines the prisoner's back—
old welts thick and knotted like blood clots—

listens a moment to his murderous heart
then pronounces him fit for punishment.
The walls grow grayer as the convict's strapped,

naked, to the trestle, his body tilted
to ease the flogger's task. His head
hangs over a bucket that reeks

of yesterday's victim's vomit. The "cat,"
they call the lash made of three leather thongs,
because it slices skin like claws. "One,"

the warden chants, like a cantor, and the cat
rises and falls. "Two . . . three . . ." By ten
the man's back is a horrible swirl

of crimson and purple. "Your Worship!" he cries,
"Spare me, Your Worship!" But the captain continues
his methodical count: eighteen, nineteen,

twenty, twenty-one, until Anton's brain
tilts on its axis, he feels his mother's hand
on his fevered forehead, sees his father rounding the corner

of Grachovka Street, a loaf of bread under his arm,
and Lydia, at their first meeting, looking away shyly
as he offers her a chocolate. Is there

such a thing as chocolate? Tears fill his eyes
and the room swims in cataract light—
the walls pulsing, floor rising and falling

like the deck of a ferry, the sun through the broken window
cutting the prisoner in half, the flogger
wheezing, hair stuck to his sweat-soaked brow—

and it takes him a moment to realize
it's the convict moaning, not him.
He sounds almost drunk, as if about to break

into song. Then suddenly he stretches his neck impossibly far
and retches violently. The sound
comes from such a distance, by the time

Anton recognizes it, it's almost a memory.
He looks around. His eyes feel strange in their sockets.
The convict's teeth chatter, the forked vein

in his forehead dances. "Forty-five . . . forty-six . . ."
Then Anton's out in the street, breathing hard,
eyes closed tight but still seeing

that bloody back, as he would see it long after
he'd completed his methodical census—
ten thousand prisoners questioned and categorized—

and returned home to write his treatise
on the penal system, his prose academic
because he did not dare write the truth

as he would a story. And he would see it still
next Easter in Paris, the "birthplace of civilization,"
where he'd travel for respite with Suvorin. There,

amidst *"anthropoi* girding themselves
with boa constrictors, dancing girls kicking
their legs toward heaven, acrobats, lions,

cafés chantants"—all the revelry
of Paris at night—he would dream
he was the man strapped to the trestle

and each blow drove him, and his torturer,
and those, like the pale author, who watched,
farther toward what made them human

and life unlivable. At such times he could not bear
the beauty of cathedrals, music, literature,
everything man had wrought

to avoid being reborn, and he craved
the singing lash, the soul's howls
and curses, and envied the convict

his bleeding, broken back,
wanting that incontrovertible proof
that he was not dead

and had not traveled so far in vain.

LEMONS

Kafka, Kierling Sanatorium, May 11, 1924

Each swallow scalds his throat, the lesions
on his larynx burn. There's nothing
to eat or drink but air. Skin

thin as parchment over bone,
when Max Brod visits he's revising
"A Hunger Artist." Neither mentions

that hack Fate, his trademark
irony. What they discuss
is thirst. On a scrap of paper, the only voice

he has left, he writes, "The worst
is that I cannot drink a single glass
of lemonade. But the craving itself

gives some satisfaction." Then,
of the flowers in a vase beside his bed,
"How marvelous that lilac. Even dying

it goes on guzzling." In three weeks
he'll scrawl his last words to Dr. Klopstock—
Kill me, or you are a murderer—

but today he's cheerful: the alcohol
injected into his laryngeal nerves
makes drinking seem almost possible

and he can think of nothing but lemons.
"At work there was a woman
who ate butter sandwiches every noon.

Can you imagine? I told her lemons
were the perfect food, so much sweet fructose
they confuse the tongue into thinking

they're sour." A disciple
of Jens Peter Mueller, the Danish bodybuilder,
all that winter he ate lemons

and exercised by an open window,
boasting to his diary, *The lighter I get*
the more I weigh asleep.

Now even his stories are weightless
compared to his merest dream. He smiles,
imagining Max feeding his manuscripts

to the fire, the words rising,
smoke and ash now, lighter, almost,
than air. The only words that deserve to last

are the ones that disappear
when pen touches paper . . .
"When I was young," he writes now,

"I squeezed invisible ink from a lemon
and wrote my sister a secret message."
(How little Elli's brow wrinkled

when he asked her to read the blank paper!
And how her mouth opened, like a starving bird's,
when he held the page over the candle-flame

and the words appeared . . .)
"If only I had that juice now," he adds,
"I would drink it, every drop."

QUOTATIONS

i.

(A childhood neighbor, nearly 100)

A hundred years from now, what will it matter?
Everything goes wrong—so what else is new?
I'm looking forward to lying down and dying.

When you buy a used car you're buying
another person's problems—just like marriage.
A hundred years from now will it matter

if grandchildren visit your bones? Used cars
break down. You can run on empty only so long.
I'm looking forward to lying down. Dying

is easy, it's living that's hard. The sun
goes up, the sun goes down. I won't understand
if I live to be a hundred. Nothing's the matter

with me—it's the world that's haywire.
If you can't sing, don't join the choir.
I'm looking forward to lying down and dying:

that's the only answer. I don't know the question.
Spit straight up and you'll learn all you need to know
a hundred years from now. Nothing matters.
Looking forward is lying. I'm down. I'm dying.

ii.

*(Marie Luise Kaschnitz, Karl Kraus, Japanese proverb,
Valéry, Nietzsche, Marvell, Herman Hupfeld, Santayana,
Kafka, Shakespeare, Simone Weil)*

The unlived life is light, so light.
You don't even live once. Drink and sing,
an inch before us is black night.
God made everything out of nothing

but the nothingness shows through.
If you gaze long into an abyss
the abyss will gaze back into you.
Had we but world enough, and time . . . A kiss

is just a kiss, a sigh is just a sigh.
Having been born is a bad augury
for immortality. There is a goal
but no way to it; what we call the way
is hesitation. Ripeness is all.
Salvation is consenting to die.

BEAUTY

The inside of his head was so beautiful, I tried to
hold the top of his head down.
— Jacqueline Kennedy Onassis

There was no time, no sense of before
or after, and its absence was filled
with the astonishing rose-pink rings

of his memory and passion.
There was no horror either, not yet,
only that beauty coiling around a fact

so large there was nothing she could do
but try to hold it in her hands . . .
Then time was back, a waterfall

crashing on rocks, and she was crawling
out of her seat toward the Secret
Service agent whose eyes were wild

with history. She was trying to disappear
into action, leave thought and feeling
behind her forever. But the reporter's question

hit her like an assassin's bullet
and she was back in the limousine,
cheers and waving hands

flanking their passage, a bouquet of roses
on her lap. Then the sudden stop
in the small talk, the recoil

of his last word, and once again she saw
her husband's head open up
like a strange flower . . .

And when she answered
she raised her hands, so beautiful
and small, to the top of her own skull.

HOMAGE TO JOHN CAGE

Silence is so accurate.
—Mark Rothko

Light through vaulted windows, the shadows
of elms in wind. On stage, the pianist,
hands in his lap. Still. The shadows
strumming his face, his hands. Four minutes

and thirty-three seconds of silence
so you may hear the music
of conditioned air through vents,
rustling clothes, the muffled echo

of shoes shuffling, all the sounds
the orchestra of chance performs.
The whole world is an auditorium.
But halfway through, those sounds fade

and you're lost in the labyrinth
of the ear, listening to the sea
of blood drumming the tympanum, the surf
of sound waves spiraling in the cochlea,

the neurons singing synapse. You're inside
the silence so far, your body
is the only world. So it's a shock
when someone coughs and brings you back

to this unreal room, a shadow
watching shadows, an echo
hearing echoes, like the souls
chained in Plato's cave. Your life flickers

on death's wall. What music can transform
shadow to substance, echo
to original score?
Your heart repeats its one note

and you listen harder, a musician now,
as the shadows drift
across the stage like snow
and find you silent, bereft.

LAZARUS

After the miracle, my sisters could not bear
to watch me eat, and when I spoke—
which was rare—they turned away
from my ruined mouth as if it were
the cave where I had lain four days
before Jesus called my name and I arose,
swaddled in graveclothes, my jaw strapped shut
with a knotted cloth, and eyes blinking
fiercely in the blast of light. I was no god
like Him, who has since risen
to His heavenly home, nor still a man
for I had died. My sister Mary washed
Our Lord's feet and dried them with her hair
but the odor of the tomb still clung
to me like a second skin, so she let dirt
blacken my feet to my scabby ankles
and my nails grow thick and horny
as a lizard's claws. And though Martha
burned bowls of resin and scattered
fragrant spices throughout our house,
still they could not bear to go near
their dear brother. How I wished
they would ask the question that made them
eye my blue-black skin, the bleeding sores
that mottled my face. Often the question
rose to their lips, where it became
"Aren't you hungry? Won't you eat some more?"
or "You've grown so thin, don't you need
another blanket to keep you warm?"
I ached to tell them how it felt
to witness your own disappearance,
the betrayal, one by one, of the senses
that comprise you, the swirl of snow
that, rising, drops you, numb, a stone,
into a well so deep no one can hear
the echo of your long fall. But words

failed me, or I failed them, and I raged
in silence till the day Mary passed me
on her way to market and her eyes
shifted from mine as from a stranger's.
With an animal howl, I took her wrist
and pulled her protesting down an alleyway
where the poor had heaped their garbage.
"This is what the dead eat," I said, and plunged
my fist into a rotted melon, writhing white
with maggots, and ate until the pulp
soaked my beard and streaked the dirt
caked on my robe. "Let me go!" she pleaded
but I held on until I'd sucked the last juice
from my fingers. Then I dropped her wrist
and waited for her to run away
as the children who called me names would do
when they saw me coming down their street.
But she just stood there, holding herself
as if suddenly cold, and looked at me,
my festering mouth, my weeping eye,
then threw her arms around me and cried
"Oh, Lazarus!" in a voice that pierced
my stone ear like a shaft of light. I woke,
then, from a sleep so deep and hollow
I had not known it was sleep, and stood there,
blinking. My hand rose to Mary's hair
and, famished, stroked it, my fingers trembling.
Then I held her dear head against my chest,
so she could hear my heart beating there,
divinely human, in its grave of bone,
before I let her, my sister, my savior, go.

SAINT FLAUBERT

i.

Rouen, 1829

Inching up the trellis against the hospital wall,
small hands shaking, he risks his father's anger
for the third time this morning, to see the naked

woman lying on the marble slab, her thigh
peeled back to the bone, his father's cold cigar
propped on her knee. Below him, his sister Caroline

cries in the garden, afraid he'll fall, or Father
will thrust his head out the window again and curse his son
the way he curses stray dogs that sneak in to steal

the flesh that falls on the floor. *Hush,* Gustave hisses,
then pulls himself to the sill and peers
over the ledge. Two students in bloodstained aprons lean

above the blue-mottled corpse, stroking their beards
as Dr. Flaubert points at something of interest
in her open chest. Suddenly Gustave's so light, a leaf

lifted in wind, if he let go of the fragile trellis
he would float in a slow whorl down to the soft stones
of the sidewalk and sleep there forever

with his cheek pressed gently against theirs.
But he clings to the trellis, trembling,
his sister's sobs rising toward him like a song.

ii.

Paris, 1843

December: one month until he suffers
the blazing epileptic lights that make him swoon, dead
to all but *Golden visions*, in his cabriolet

on the road between Deauville and Rouen, precisely where
a mail coach nearly kills Félicité and her parrot
in *Un Coeur Simple.* He heads a band of bohemian law students

staggering through the Latin Quarter and discourses
on the subject of love: *The most beautiful woman
is not beautiful on a dissecting table, her bowels*

draped over her face. His friends howl at this latest
example of his famous cynicism, and howl again
at the brothel where, as always, he ostentatiously selects

the ugliest of the girls, this time a fat Breton
with jowls and a wen. *Come, my little cow,* he jokes,
and prods her up the stairs with his umbrella

to the dark room where he will crawl onto her, eyes open,
beret cocked to one side, the only light the red tip
of the cigar burning between his clenched teeth.

iii.

Croisett, 1853

All day long he has been falling in love
with Emma's fate, the arsenic in a kiss,
and now he sits exhausted at his table,

midges and moths fluttering around the candle,
and writes to the mistress he refuses to visit.
It is a delicious thing to write, whether well

or badly—to be no longer yourself but to move
in an entire universe of your own creating. Today,
for instance, man and woman, lover and beloved,

I rode in a forest on an autumn afternoon
under the yellow leaves, and I was also the horse,
the leaves, the wind, the words my people spoke,

even the red sun that made them half shut
their love-drowned eyes. He shuts his own eyes,
the dark flickering with the after-image of candlelight,

and thinks *Louise*, luxuriating in her name
as in a lover's bed. They are making love quietly,
so her daughter will not wake. When he opens his eyes

he isn't sure he hasn't slept. A moth is crawling
beside the scalpel that earlier that day dissected
Emma's beautiful stupidity. He brushes it away,

leaving an ash-gray smudge on the page. *Is this pride*
or piety? he continues. *Is it a silly overflow*
of exaggerated self-satisfaction, or is it really

a vague and noble religious instinct?

iv.

Nohant, 1876

Her funeral was like a chapter in one of her books,
he will write, later, to Turgenev. But now
there is no such thing as literature: he stands

ankle deep in mud in the village cemetery, the rain
dripping from the broad brim of his hat, weeping
(he will later say) *like a child*, and climbs

toward the window again, afraid this time the trellis
will not hold. Caroline, Mother, Louise
and now George Sand. *What a splendid man she was,*

and what a woman! Turgenev will write back. Yawning,
a boy in a soiled cassock swings a censer to and fro
while the curé mocks her life with prayers. But Gustave

doesn't hear. He is listening to the men straddling the gravetrestles,
their sacred grunts and groans, as they strain
to lower the casket carefully into its hole.

v.

Croisett, 1876

This time he's chosen the most beautiful woman
he can imagine, plain and celibate, a saint
to match his beloved legend, Julian the Hospitaller, who

lay chastely down atop a leper, mouth to mouth,
breast to breast, thigh to thigh, to warm
his snake-cold skin and so rose swooning into Heaven

clasped in his Savior's arms. But Félicité's a heretic
who prays to Loulou, her stuffed, worm-eaten parrot,
reasoning *God wouldn't choose a dove to speak for Him*

*since doves can't talk. And isn't that bird
in the colorprint above the baptismal font
emerald-green and its wings tipped red?* There is a logic

to faith, and it has led him, exhausted and tearful,
to the final sentence of her story. All week long
Gustave has been old maid and parrot, the priest

carrying the body of Christ through the streets
of Pont-l'Évêque, the censer-bearers,
the poppy-red canopy held aloft by four churchwardens,

the crowd which follows, the clamor of churchbells,
the altar of repose with its vases of foxgloves,
hydrangea, lilies, and peonies, even the monstrance,

that gold sun, on the lace altar cloth. And now
he is her shallow breathing and the fly-specked window
through which she smells the blue cloud of incense

before she closes her eyes and he sees
the golden breast and lapis lazuli poll
of Loulou descend on him, its beak opening to bless

his long pilgrimage with its screech.

NEVER

Norfork River, Arkansas

The grateful collapse of muscles
exhausted by pleasure. The ache

of calves, thighs, back, and casting arm
almost sexual. I lie on the bank,

six fat trout in my creel, the smell
of wild mint, and wind just barely stirring

the tall grass. I can't bear the fact
that one day I will no longer

see or hear or touch. Never again
this river, its song of here

becoming there. Never fog lifting
the hem of its skirt, nor trout

sifting like silt in green dark.
Never sunlight refracted, quicksilver,

in pools, a lone cloud drifting
downstream like a raft,

nor fishermen wading so far out
they're half river and their talk

is water over rocks. And never, even,
the word *never*, its syllables so sad

and delicious in my mouth . . .

VIETNAM VETERANS MEMORIAL

for Andrea and Susanne Dunn

For years you were only names
    in your father's letters,
words I attached to vague memories

of two small girls playing pat-a-cake
    one summer a lifetime ago.
Driving to New Jersey to see your parents

I barely thought of you. I was thinking
    about two friends who died
before you were even born. In Washington

I stopped to read their names
    carved in granite as dark
as history. I wanted the comfort

stone offers, the good lie
    of forever,
but when I looked at the black wall,

the sun chiselled the names of the dead
    on my reflected face
and I turned away, knowing

we cannot survive what does not end.
    But the next day you rose
from the past, your faces so wholly

beyond mere survival
    and continuum, I thought of
resurrection, incarnation,

language I abandoned
    twenty years ago. Andrea, Susanne,
my friends are only names now,

names that drift like clouds
    in the wall's dark sky,
just as your names, miles away,

drift across the darkening yard
    as your parents call you
to dinner and their love.

For us, the living,
    there is no other monument.
Just the air, the breath,

our names passing between us.

STAR LEDGER

in memory of L.H.

A dozen years ago, my student still,
you watched streetlights and stars mottle
your rainstruck windshield into waterlilies
and drove through that dream of Giverny

into a parked car. When you woke, headache
stitched into place, you knew how much beauty
could hurt . . . For years I told this story
to the students who followed you, to make

its easy point. What did I know then
about beauty, the pain of words colliding
with desire, the shattered glass and twisted steel
of loss? Today I read your poems again.
Lynda, I wish I could tell you how beautiful
their light is through the killing rain.

AGAINST SUNSETS

The dust can't keep its secret—
the sun, going down, soaks the sky
with the red fact of it. But that's
not clue enough for some lovers:
they credit the sun for what
the dust has done to it
and sip champagne in its honor.

Let them have their sunsets. I'll take
the moment after, when shadows stretch
away from the house and the day
goes out of us like a sigh.
That still moment, breathless,
before evening skins the light.

Everything's more precious then.
For instance, tonight,
the kiss-shape your lips made
as you took from the shelf a book
you hadn't read in years
and prepared to blow off the dust.

NOCTURNE

*after "Effet de nuit," a pastel by William Degouve
de Nuncques*

Why look beyond
    the horizon? Compared to the lit
      windows of these houses
scattered across the far meadow

the moon is a pale reminder
    of what's missing
      in this sky bruised haze-blue
by the coming dark. Behind these windows

lovers like us pass the last hours
    before the long night,
      talking quietly,
carefully, the way they close doors

to rooms where children are dreaming.
    They know how fragile
      their solid houses are, how already
the river has turned vague as fog

in preparation to vanish. Come here.
    Put your arms around me
      while we watch that other river, the sky,
swell its banks, wave by wave,

and flood the world. Soon
    everything will be shadow
      and mist. Everything
except these lights, which the dark,

deepening, only brightens
    until they're all that's left,
      our private stars,
this constellation we'll christen *home*.

THE PROPOSITION OF ANY RIVER

i.

The proposition of any river
is *surrender*. The tug of current

at the will, the lure
of oblivion, so tempting

when each stroke of the paddle
burns in our shoulders

and August heat laps at us,
dissolving the day

into perpetual noon. It's impossible
to paddle further: we belong

to the river now, flotsam
on the surface of its dream . . .

ii.

Later, we lie in the shade of poplars,
too tired to talk. Bees hum around us,

a language water could understand,
and leaves flicker in the sun

like rocks under quick current.
I close my eyes and the light

is still there, licking at my eyelids,
and the earth beneath me

drifts and eddies like a river.
I'm almost asleep. Then you turn

and kiss me, the smell of your hair
an undertow that pulls me

all the way down.

STARDUST

Tonight, the wind winds down the hill
to the house we refuse, for a moment,

to enter. So what if we're cold, our skin
stippled with goosebumps, and the firewood

is waiting for the match? We linger
a moment longer, looking up

at what reminds us we are not the first
to stand here pausing before this house

nor the last. Time is as vast
as this sky, and as dark,

yet we are made of stardust, the calcium
in our bones and iron in our blood

the fallout of the first supernovas,
and the wind, that original music,

still strums the leaves in our yard
and the woods beyond. Its melody will last

almost forever, yet we listen as if
we will never hear it again. In a minute

we'll go inside and light the fire
then hold each other, as others after us

will hold each other, and watch the temporary
take flight, the sunlight that wound the logs

escaping at last, sparks rising from the flames
like stars returning home.